THE PATHWAY TO HONOR

By

EMMANUEL O. AFOLABI

Copyright © 2016. All rights reserved.

No part of this publication may be reproduced, stored in a retrieval system or transmitted in any way by any means, electronic, mechanical, photocopy, recording or otherwise, without the prior permission of the author except as provided by USA copyright law.

All characters appearing in this work are fictitious. Any resemblance to real persons, living or dead, is purely coincidental.

All scripture quotations are taken from the Kings James version (KJV & NKJV) the Holy Bible, except where otherwise stated.

The opinions expressed by the author are not necessarily those of Revival Waves of Glory Books & Publishing.

Published by Revival Waves of Glory Books & Publishing

PO Box 596| Litchfield, Illinois 62056 USA

www.revivalwavesofgloryministries.com

Revival Waves of Glory Books & Publishing is committed to excellence in the publishing industry.

Book design Copyright © 2016 by Revival Waves of Glory Books & Publishing. All rights reserved.

Published in the United States of America

FOREWORD

Bro. Afolabi's new book titled "The Pathway to Honor" is well prepared and gives insight into receiving the honor of God through righteousness and commitment to our calling as Christians. He distinguished between the world's honor and honor received from God. Honor from God is based on faithfulness, commitment and righteousness of the individual. There is a difference from seeking honor and being honored, the author therefore advised for one to be wary of taking or receiving worldly honors which often are coated with conditionality.

Honor from God or of God requires consistent walking with the Lord and working for God. The author further highlighted four principles for greatness: courage, desire, persistence and time utilization. He further refreshes our memory of men of faith who by virtue of their walk with God were honored by both men and God. One thing that is common to them all, they learned to hold on firmly to the Rock of Ages. Faithfulness promotes and enhances honor, according to the word of God from Proverbs chapter 22:29,

"Seest thou a man diligent in his business? He shall stand before kings; he shall not stand before mean men."

The pathway to honor may appear rough and difficult. However, we are not alone; we have God's assurance of His presence in our journey of life. The current effort of Brother Afolabi as detailed in this book will be a source of motivation for Christians unto every good work for the Lord and humanity. I hereby congratulate the author for allowing himself to be used of God, hence, a source of blessing to the body of Christ.

    Rev. Dapo Longe
    Senior Pastor/Zonal Superintendent
    Foursquare Gospel Church in Nigeria
    Jakande Zonal Headquarters Church
    Jakande Estate, Isolo.

ACKNOWLEDGMENT

Glory is unto God, great things He has done in helping me to accomplish the desire to finish this work. I sincerely acknowledge the contribution of the Zonal Superintendent of Foursquare Gospel Church Jakande Estate Zone, Rev. Dapo Longe who wrote the foreword, for his interest in seeing that the project is a huge success, my beloved Resident Pastor P. O. Adekanle who is my project supervisor and wrote about the book. He indeed increased my enthusiasm, bolstered my morale and motivated me to work harder. My thanks go to my daughter, Margret Oreoluwa Afolabi, who used her valuable time to edit the book.

I also appreciate the contribution of a few friends who showed interest in this work.

It is my prayer that the Lord will reward them all in abundance.

DEDICATION

I dedicate this book exclusively to the Lord Holy Spirit who inspired me to put up this work. Thank you, Holy Spirit.

PROLOGUE

The Holy Bible (NKJV) The Bible contains the mind of God, the state of man, the way of salvation, the doom of sinners, and the happiness of believers, its doctrines are holy, its precepts are bindings, its histories are true and its decisions are immutable. Read it to be wise, believe it to be safe, and practice it to be holy. It contains light to direct you, food to support you, and comfort to cheer you.

It is the traveler's map, the pilgrim's staff, the pilot's compass, the soldier's sword, and the Christian's charter. Here paradise is restored, heaven opened, and the gates of hell disclosed.

CHRIST is its grand subject, and the glory of God its end. It should fill the memory, rule the heart, and guide the feet. Read it slowly, frequently, and prayerfully. It is a mine of wealth, a paradise of story, and a river of pleasure. It is given for life, will be opened at the judgment, and be remembered forever. It involves the highest responsibility, will reward the greatest labour and will condemn all who triple with the sacred contents? Extracts from Gideon pocket Bible, the Holy Bible (NKJV, KJV), Oxford Advanced Learner's Dictionary 6th Edition and English Mini Dictionary.

INTRODUCTION

The Oxford Advanced Learner's Dictionary (6th Edition) defined Honor as a great respect and admiration for somebody, a good reputation, respect from other people, an award, official title given to somebody as a reward for something they have done. But God's perspective of honor differs because He will honor those who honor Him in fears and obedience to His instruction. The saying of God Almighty in the book of First Samuel readily comes to mind.

"Therefore the Lord God of Israel says I said indeed that your house and the house of your father would walk before Me forever. But now the Lord says: Far be it from Me, for those who honor Me, I will honor and those who despise Me shall be highly esteemed." 1 Samuel 2:30.

Since the true place and pathway to honor is in God, our focus, therefore must be upon God to reward us. When you stand out for God you are not only going to be a winner, but a winner with dividend. He rewards everyone according to how his work shall be, if God penciled you down for honor nobody can dishonor you. However, it is your departure from holiness and righteousness like Eli and his children that will bring dishonor. Friend whenever you cease listening to instruction, then you will stray from the words of knowledge.

"Cease listening to instruction, My son, And you will stray from the words of knowledge." Prov. 19:27
"He who keeps instruction is in the way of life. But he who refuses correction goes astray." Prov. 10:17.

So therefore, those who aspire to be honored by God must renounce the unrighteousness and act of shame, not walking in craftiness, not handling what you profess to be truth deceitfully, thereby commending yourself in every man's conscience. Then you will make it to God's list of men of honor.

Honor sought from men is a temporary admiration and respect that will soon be short lived, because whenever you decide to stand for the truth, whereby you refuse to compromise your standard, the end result is that you will be regarded as a rebellious person who stands to oppose the constituted authority. In vain, your behavior or action will tantamount to recalcitrance. So the honor conferred on you will be brought to disrepute.

Most men, if not all, look for public advertisement. Stop advertising yourself or singing your own praises. Let God advertise you.

"It is not good to eat much honey. So to seek one's own glory is not glory." Prov. 25:27.

In your quest for honor, you must allow this mind be in you which was also in Christ Jesus who humble Himself and became obedient to the point of death.

"Let this mind be in you which was also in Christ Jesus. Who, being in the form of God, did not consider it robbery to be equal with God, but make Him no reputation, taking the form of a bond servant, and coming in the likeness of men: And being found in appearance as a man? He humbled Himself and became obedient to the point of death, even the death of the cross. Therefore God also has highly exalted Him and given Him the name which is above every name; that at the name of Jesus every knee should bow, of those in heaven: and those on the earth, and of those under the earth, and that every tongue should confess that Jesus Christ is Lord to the glory of God the Father." Phil. 2:5-11.

Jesus himself said in the book of John 13:15, "I have given you an example that you should do as I have done to you." Are you subject to authority? Do you adhere strictly to instruction in your little corner that the Lord has placed you, in your office, or business place or ministry in the vineyard of God? Listen to this and take hold fast to it.

"Take fast hold of instruction: let her not go, keep her, for she is your life." Prov. 4:13.

When you allow your heart to retain instruction, discretion shall keep you. So shall you find favor and good understanding in the sight of God and men, thereby avail yourself to a level plain ground to walk upon on the pathway to honor.

Let God take His rightful position in your life, by constantly honoring Him in carrying out your assigned responsibilities diligently and faithfully and assuredly at the time appointed you will be decorated with medals.
As we journey through the pathway to honor, realize this fact that in God is the true place of an enduring honor.
Shalom. **Emmanuel O. Afolabi**

CHAPTER 1

THE PATHWAY TO HONOR

The pathway to honor is in God. Honor generally means giving public praise, an award or a title to somebody for something he/she has done (e.g.) Nobel Prize, National award, etc.) However, God Almighty is the only one who can indeed define the "honor code." 1 Sam. 2:30, John 5:44.

God honors people according to their righteous endeavor and motive behind whatsoever they do. His eyes sees beyond the intent of our heart and He recompenses everyone accordingly.

"With a pure heart, you shall show yourself pure, with the forward you will show yourself forward." Psalm 18:26.

The righteous God will reward us according to the righteousness of our works in His sight.

"Therefore the Lord has recompensed me according to my righteousness: According to the cleanness of my hands in His sight." Psalm 18:24.

The word of God stands and sure He will not change His stand regarding His word to accommodate us. The pathway to honor is a path of righteous living and obedient. The Psalmist asked the question: **"LORD, who may abide in your tabernacle? Who may dwell in your holy hill? He who walks uprightly. And works righteousness. And speaks the truth in his heart." Psalm 15:1&2.**

"The Lord rewards me according to my righteousness, according to the cleanness of my hands. He has recompensed me. For I have kept the ways of the LORD. And have no wickedly departed from my God. For all His judgments were before me; and I did not put away His statutes from me. I was also blameless before Him. And I kept myself from any iniquity. **Therefore the LORD has recompensed me according to my righteousness. According to the cleanness of my hands in His sight."** Psalm 18:20-24.

Remember that the Almighty God has no favoritism with anyone; hence, the principle of God's own 'honor code' must be followed strictly. The fear of the Lord is the beginning of wisdom. When you walk in the fear of the Lord, then you will apply your mind to the understanding that will cause you to find the favor of God and man. Jesus advised us in the book of John about the type of honor we should desire.

"How can you believe, who receive honor from one another and do not seek the honor that comes from the only God." John 5:14.

In your given assignment, are you faithful in discharging your duties? Nevertheless, you shall likewise get your reward.

But on the pathway to honor, faithfulness is the key to Godly kind of honor.

"And he said to him. Well done, good servant; because you were faithful in a very little, have authority over ten cities." Luke 19:17.

My dear reader, do not despise your little beginning. Your faithfulness and obedience in carrying out your assigned responsibility in the fear of the Lord without anyone monitoring you, though nobody recognizes you now, be rest assured your faithfulness and righteous doings will be compensated. He that sees in the secret shall reward you openly. People may be looking down at you, or treating you unjustly, do not cast away your confidence which has great reward, for you have need of endurance, hence you are persuaded as you are doing the will of God in your given assignment and undertaking. Do not be intimidated, but be courageous. "For yet a little while, And He who is coming will come and will not tarry."

"Therefore do not cast away your confidence, which has great reward. For you have need of endurance, so that after you done the will of God. You may receive the promise. For yet a little while, And He who is coming will come and will not tarry." Heb. 10:35-37.

You cannot surpass God when it comes to blessing. He is the author of true blessing and enduring honor. So whenever He purposed in Himself to shower a blessing upon you, it becomes irrevocable. "STICK TO GOD and you will definitely arrive at your level of your desire.

Beloved in the pathway to honor, God has strategically positioned you to fulfill your God ordained destiny in your current place of work, business etc., What is required of you is your dedication to duties and faithfulness most especially in your dealing with others. God will reward your motive and action. Your undertaking will be put on the measuring scale of God's own standard of rewarding productivity either in secular or spiritual.

In the pathway to honor, you should make up your mind to accommodate the following and prepare to live with them:

I) **Shame and confusion:** You may be ridiculed, disgraced and despised in the cause of your dealing with others, but He that resides inside of you shall show-forth at the time appointed even when you don't realize or thinking that you are alone. He watches over you.

"Instead of your shame you shall have double honor, and instead of confusion they shall rejoice in their portion. Therefore, on their land they shall possess double everlasting joy shall be theirs." Isaiah 61:7.

II) **Humility and fear of God:** Humble yourself in the sight of God always and in due season He will exalt you. The fear of the Lord is the beginning of wisdom.

"By humility and the fear of the Lord, Are riches and honor and life." Prov. 22:4.

As you humble yourself in the fear of the Lord in your journey through the pathway to honor, assuredly the tripartite blessings of riches, honor and life shall be available to you in Jesus Name Amen.

CHAPTER 2

HONOR SOUGHT FROM MEN

Honor sought from men is vain glory that will not last, because it failed to take the process and principle of success and honor. It must surely have a short life.

When you embark on the journey of singing your own praises or advertising yourself, you are simply drumming up vain glory that would eventually bring disgrace. The only thing that can take you to the top is when you follow the principle of success and honor which is faithfulness. But when you prefer compromise, it will only lead you to failure. But be reminded that the children of this world are wiser in their ways. Your line of operation, then will be under the law of 'Nothing goes for anything'. If you pave your way to the top, you must be ready to sell out your conscience, and then become a tool in the hand of the enemy.

Let's see how men honor the Lord Jesus Christ, on His way to Jerusalem for the Passover feast. They brought to Jesus the colt, and they cast their garments upon the colt and set Jesus thereon. As he went, they spread their clothes on the way. When He was descent of the Mount of Olives, the whole multitude of the disciples began to rejoice and praise God with a loud voice for all the mighty works that they had seen. **"Saying blessed be the King that comes in the name of the Lord. Peace in heaven, and glory in the highest."** The same people that honored Him, were the one shouting crucify Him, crucify Him. Luke 20:35-38.

Another perfect example is that of David. After the defeat of Goliath, King Saul promoted him to become the Commander of the Israelite Army. No sooner, had the women began to sing the praises of David, saying Saul killed a thousand, David killed ten thousands that the spirit of jealousy entered into Saul, saying, they have ascribed more honor to David than himself and what next if not for David to take over the whole kingdom. Then he sought to kill David. He eventually demoted David from the position of Commander to Captain, thereby stripping him of the honor earlier conferred on him. That is an honor from men. The moment you stand for the truth or began to out-shine them they we see you as a threat, and without wasting time you will be dishonored. 1 Sam 1:7-13.

It takes a great prize to retain men's honor, which are dishonesty, compromise and deceit. But the word of God will never change, it abides forever. Therefore, be careful, because when a man compromises about his principles, downfall becomes imminent.

"The Lord brings the counsel of the nations to nothing; He makes the plans of the people of no effect. The counsel of the Lord stands forever. The plans of His heart to all generations." Psalm 33:10-11.

CHAPTER 3

THE ODDS ON THE PATHWAY TO HONOR

Esther shows how the Almighty God can save His people against the most overwhelming odds, even using an inexperienced young lady to change national history. Esther availed herself to save His people from destruction and give His people reason to celebrate. Her case proved that a humble girl from God's people can attain national importance. Faithfulness to God can be expressed by serving faithfully in a government establishment and in other places including foreign government. Serving in responsible positions calls for faithfulness to God, even in your current position with the assigned responsibility.

Dear readers, remember this always in the course of your duties either to God or to man. God works in history to honor responsible and faithful action. God uses honor and celebration to reposition people with increase chances for service.

The case of Mordecai rightly comes to mind on how God rewarded his faithfulness. Esther 10:2&3. While you walk through the pathway to honor, your burning desire to impact your world must not be put-off until you fulfill your God ordained destiny. Don't allow the hedge of the protection around you to be cracked, hold firmly to Him. He will teach, instruct and guide you with His eyes until you are decorated with medals.

In the book of Psalm 32:8, God declared what He would do if we allow Him to lead the way. He will teach, instruct and guide us to achieve our burning desire. With God all things are possible to them that believe. Even when you think you are alone on the pathway to honor, He watches over you. His grace equally creates a limitless boundary of operation. Thanks be to God for His active involvement in all that concern or affect us. In the book of Romans 12:6, it is evidently clear that God has given each and every one of us the ability to do certain things well. In spite of the ability availed to us, He reassured us that He will constantly teach, instruct and guide us with His eyes until we arrive at our level of desire.

Before you can become agent of change in your world, you need to be consistent with your inborn desire to impact the life of others; hence your consistent lifestyle must be the mind-set that has God at the center.

When the center is firm, the other areas will be in shape. But when the center can no longer hold, every other area will fall apart and you will not be able to impact your world positively. You must also dutifully and diligently carry out the assignment given to you either by God or man. You should put all that is required into it to fulfill the assignment. God will always reward faithful action.

God knows the potential he has deposited in you, capable of withstanding any pressure from any corner; hence He placed you in a strategic position that you may become His battle ax. The case of Esther is a perfect example of how God can use whosoever surrendered to Him. Esther became God's battle ax for the Lord in the Land of Shushan and in the lives of the Jews.

God used her to avert bloodshed in Shushan. In the same way God is expecting you to be His battle ax in wherever and in any position you may find yourself, to stand in the gap for the people around you. God has confidence in what you can do in your current position. 'SO DO NOT DISAPPOINT HIM.' Esther, the little girl in the foreign land, determined that even if it cost her life, she would fight to the finish.**" If I perish I perish." Esther 4:16.** The God that watches over her rose to the occasion, though, working behind the scene until she was crowned with victory and decorated with medals.

In the pathway to honor, you should add more value to your life. Don't be static. Train yourself with something more you can do to improve yourself. Whatever your hands find to do, you should do it excellently. Let your heart burn with new ideas on how to serve people better. People count in place of honor. Because some people come into your life as a 'blessing' other come in as a 'lesson'. You need both of them.

Learn something new about your trade or profession that will tremendously improve your life. Think of better ways to serve people. Who says you cannot be honored? It is your life; and you alone can make it come out the way it ought. 'If you have not experienced failure, it means you have not attempted a new thing'. Failure is an opportunity to start again until success is achieved. Don't be scared of failure, but be prepared and have a mind-set that you will make it. Success depends on how you handle failure, and with strong determination you will surely arrive at the platform of success.

Your current position is your opportunity, make it right, and see your life move from one level of glory to another. Hold firmly to God's instruction as you walk on the pathway to honor and you will be unstoppable.

"The fear of the Lord is the beginning of knowledge. But fools despise wisdom and instruction." Prov. 1:7.

Self-confidence is another virtue we must exhibit on the pathway to honor, don't lose confidence in yourself. We start losing faith in our abilities and cut down our activities out of fear that we may fail. A baby grows by self-confidence and efforts, right from birth and then to crawling, standing, walking and running. Self-confidence is inbuilt in the growth process and only when we grow old do we gradually lose self-confidence.

Self-confidence is inherent in our structure, while fear is an acquired complex.

"For God has not given us the spirit of fear, but of power, and of love, and of a sound mind." 2 Tim. 1:7.

The top is possible to all and the ladder of success does not care who climbs it. You cannot climb with your bare hands and if you jump, you will come down, but if you have a ladder to climb you are sure to arrive at your desired level. One thing is clear, preparation is not easy, the human nature hates pressure, nobody wants to experience hard times, but it is a necessity.

No road in life is free of challenges. There is no glory without a story to tell. Peradventure God is giving you a story attached to His glory and honor.

The obstacles placed at every distance are your gateway to your significance and advancement; crisis are materials for success, converting problems to prospect, obstacles for miracles, trails to testimonies, thereby moving from zero level to hero level.

Life itself is not theoretical, but practical. Your obstacles and trials, most times, are God designed to usher you into fulfillment. If you dodge challenges, you may end up aborting the change which the challenges are orchestrated to provoke.

If Joseph and Daniel did not go through the school of challenges and dodged it, what do you think would have become their God ordained destiny? Joseph faced the challenges of his life head on, he faced the rigors of being dumped into the pit by his own brothers, sold to the Mediante Merchant, got to Egypt meeting Potsphar's wife who lied against him, he was sentenced to jail for an offense he knew nothing about, and later met the butler who mentioned him to Pharaoh. Joseph eventually became Prime Minister in Egypt. Our God is just. He has a way of taking us to our throne, using problems to introduce us to those that are to help us.

There can be no profit without conflict, and there can be no promotion without opposition.

"But it so happened, when Sanballat heard that we were rebuilding the wall, that he was furious and very indignant and mocked the Jews." Nehemiah 4:1.

If Daniel had ganged-up with the mischief makers and was not thrown in the lion's den, how could he have proved that he had a superior God? That singular incident announced God's superiority and significance in his life to the whole world? God's sometimes allows certain challenges to come into man's life because he requires such to push him to the next level.

Opportunity and crisis are like Siamese twins; you cannot enjoy one and wish the other away. So do not pray for problems not to happen, because whether you pray against or not, crisis will always come, it is part of life.

The challenges of life are never intended to destabilize you, they are your resolve, test of your faith and to teach you how to think and generate enough courage and solutions for both complex and non-complex situations. Whenever you find a solution to problems it brings further advancement to life and it will enhance your development. If there are no challenges, there can be no change. If you want to be great so be ready to solve great problems. The victors are war heroes, until you have been involved in a battle you cannot be decorated with medals. **"Hard times**

are designed to build personalities. So never be blown away by wind. .."

Do not be frightened when you come across problems. In your pursuit, do not fret either, but confront them, for whatever you cannot confront you will not be able to conquer. Find out what is next. Every challenge is a key to opening a new door. Do not wish problem never came. Had Joseph escaped the prison or had Daniel disappeared before they could throw him into the lion's den, you would not have heard of them. Do not allow anything to take you away from God, as you resolve to serve God more, He will satisfy you early with His mercy that you may rejoice and be glad all your days.

"O satisfies us early with your mercy that we may rejoice and be glad all our days." Psalm 90:14.

Since the pathway to honor is in God, you must have a mind-set that you want to attain to the place of honor. "As a man thinketh in his heart so is he." Adopting the right kind of mind-set is central to winning in all life endeavors. There is a world of difference between I CAN and I CAN'T. And one of these two is chosen and engraved in the mind as we respond to life challenges. When you think positively, you will feel more in control and you will find a solution without realizing it; you mobilize all your senses and system to bring about success. Your normal word will be I can make it. We can do this... Let's give it our best shot... When you think negatively such as I can't do it, your senses and system will work against you, and you will be comfortable with the words like I can't do it, we can't make it, or what is the point?

Take note of these four principles of attainments which the heroes of the past exhibited before they were decorated.

I) COURAGE: The English Mini Dictionary defined courage as the ability to control fear when facing danger or pain. It takes a high degree of courage to be successful, courage is what helps you to stick your neck out and to do something extra-ordinary, when you could easily stay put in your present position and live in your comfort zone. Courage is the ladder in which you must climb if you must reach the level of desire.

"If you faint in the day of adversity, your strength is small." Prov. 24:10.

"Only be strong and very courageous, that you may observe to do according to all the law which Moses My servant commanded you, do not turn from it to the right hand or to the left, that you may proper wherever you go." Joshua 1:7.

II) DESIRE: The English Mini Dictionary defined desire as a strong feeling of wanting something. "Success" results from focusing the full power of all you are in what you have a burning desire to achieve". Wilfred Peterson and Napoleon Hill said, "The starting point of all achievement is desire." Paul Mayer added his dimension, in the following words. "Whatever you vividly imagine, ardently desire; sincerely believe and enthusiastically act upon must inevitably come to pass." The place of desire in the achievement of success or breakthrough in any endeavor cannot be over emphasized.

The Bible confirms "That if we delight ourselves in the LORD. He will give us the desire of your heart." Psalm 27:4.

III) PERSISTENCE: The English Mini Dictionary defined persistence as to continue doing something in spite of difficulty or opposition. Money grows on the tree of persistence. (Japanese Proverb) Success as a whole process that requires 'Stay on'. The slogan 'press on" has solved and always will solve the problems of the human race. Nothing in the whole world can take the place of persistence.

"But may the God of all grace, who called us to His eternal glory by Christ Jesus, after you have suffered a while, perfect, establish, strengthen and settle you." 1 Peter 5:10.

IV) TIME UTILISATION: The English Mini Dictionary defined time as the continuing progress of existence and events in the past, present and future. If life is measured in terms of time, then wasted time is like life abused. Time is money, but only if well utilized. Bad time utilization is a loss of money. Charles Richard said, "Do not be fooled by the calendar. There are only as many days in the year as you make use of. One man gets only a week's value out of a year, while another man gets a full year's value out of a week." Therefore, take time to work; it is the price of success. Take time to think; it is the source of power. Take time to read; it is the foundation of knowledge. Take time to pray; it is the Christian's vital breath.

"Do not love sleep, lest you come to poverty. Open your eyes, and you will be satisfied with bread." Prov. 20:13. "Wealth makes many friends, But the poor is separated from his friend." Prov. 19:4.

'Nobody waits until night looking for honor, it is usually sought for in the noonday. Since work is the process of our lives, whatever your hand finds to do, therefore do it excellently well, so in the day of recognition you may be considered among others and be singled out for honor'. "He who has a slack hand becomes poor. But the hand of the diligent makes rich." Prov. 10:4. "HARD WORK

PAYS AND YIELDS DIVIDEND WHEN THE STRENGTH IS CHANNELED THROUGH THE RIGHT PATH."

Joseph, Daniel and Esther practiced these principles in one way or the other as they faced different challenges on their pathway to honor. But they never strayed away from His presence nor refrained from His instructions. When you follow hard after God. The sky will be your limit in regards to success and honor.

"Yes, if you cry out for understanding. If you seek for her as silver. And search for her as hidden treasure. Then you will understand the fear of the LORD. And find the knowledge of God." Prov. 2:3-5.

Honor will reposition you for added responsibilities like Joseph, Daniel and Mordecia. If you are not willing, nor ready to assume higher responsibilities, then the pathway to the Godly kind of honor should be avoided. Because to whom much is given, much is expected. God will not put His premium on anyone who is negligent to duties. As you face the challenges of life as they come, 'Stay on' and be diligent in your assigned responsibility. 'Whosoever desires to eat an egg in the midst of a stone, would not be bothered on what happened to the edge of an ax' (e.g. Persistence). I see you therefore fulfilling your God ordained destiny in Jesus Name.

CHAPTER 4

THE BIBLICAL MEN OF HONOR AND HOW THEY COME ABOUT IT

Men of honor have their trying period as they walk through the pathway to honor, obstacles and challenges are part and parcel of the prize of honor.

But these men of honor hold firmly to the Rock of Ages and they eventually arrive at the decorating point. Also remember in all your assigned responsibility that without battle is no crown. The Book of Genesis chapters 37 - 44 gave details of Joseph's life and experiences from one stage to another before he appeared to Pharaoh who decorated him with medals.

His life ordeals began with petty jealousy over his coat of many colors and with the special treatment showered on him by Israel far and above other children of his, because Joseph happened to be the son of his old age. His brothers did not take it kindly with this gesture, whereby they refused to speak peaceably with Joseph. He further aggravated hatred from his brothers when he told them about his dreams and how they all bowed down before him. The Bible recorded that they hated him even more. Genesis 37: 5.

With this provoking revelation about what awaited them in the event that the dream comes to pass, they all marveled at his word, saying among themselves to Joseph shall you indeed reign over us? In the process of time, Joseph began to wax stronger and growing in age to carry out some lesser assignment without monitoring. On this fateful day, his Father, Israel called to Joseph and sent him to go to seek the welfare of his brothers who went to feed the flocks in She-hem. In obedience, he proceeded on the journey to seek for his brothers. After much wandering about in the wilderness, he got assistance from someone who directed him to where he could locate his brothers.

When they set their eyes upon him afar off, they said to one another, here comes the dreamer! They agreed among themselves to kill him and cast him into some pit, and we shall say some wild beast have devoured him. 'We shall see what will become of his dreams'. Wicked counsel, but God frustrated their counsel.

"Who frustrates the signs of the babblers, and drives diviners mad, who turns wise men backward, and makes their knowledge foolishness." Isaiah 44:25.

"There are many plans in a man's heart. Nevertheless the Lord's counsel that will stand." Prov. 19:21.

The Lord caused Reuben to plead with his brethren, saying shed no blood, but cast him into this pit which is in the wilderness and do not lay a hand on him, that he may deliver him out of their hands and bring him back to his father.

The plan of God for Joseph was not to be returned to his Father, but to continue his journey of life to fulfill his God ordained destiny, hence Reuben wondered away at the time Joseph was sold out.

They stripped Joseph of his coat of many colors, dumped into a dry well, eventually sold to the Ishmaelite coming from Gilead to Egypt. This entire thing happened in the absence of Reuben because God had a better plan for Joseph. When he got to Egypt, the Medianites sold Joseph to Portiphar, an officer of Pharaoh and the Captain of the guard; because God was with Joseph. He blessed the household of Portiphat for Joseph's sake. Portiphat set Joseph over his house, because he realized that God was with him. As he was settling down to life in Egypt, another challenge arose. He was accused, and sentenced to prison for an offense, he knew nothing about. He was put in the same prison where the king's prisoners were confined.

But God caused him to find favor with the keeper of the prison who put everything under the care of Joseph. The chief butler and baker were put in the same custody because Pharaoh was not pleased with them. It came to pass that both the butler's and baker's dreams happened in one night. The butler narrated his dream to Joseph, who gave him the interpretation that in three days, he will be reinstated to his duty post. The baker also told Joseph about his dream, but the interpretation wasn't favorable, saying in three days Pharaoh will behead him and his body will be hung on a tree and birds will eat up his flesh. Actually, so it was after the third day. Despite Joseph's request of the butler to make mention of him to Pharaoh, he was forgotten in the prison for yet another two years.

At the age of thirty, God showed up to fulfill his purpose in the life of Joseph. He caused Pharaoh to dream twice that none among his wise men could interpret it. Pharaoh was angry with his wise men and sentenced them all for execution. It was there, then the butler remembered Joseph in the prison. So he told Pharaoh about Joseph and how he could interpret dreams, because he had interpreted his dream and it came to pass.

Immediately, Pharaoh summoned Joseph to appear before him. He was cleaned up, and dressed with fine linen cloth before he appeared to Pharaoh. At the time appointed for his honor, he appeared before Pharaoh. He spoke to Joseph about how he had dreamt twice and that no one could interpret it. But I have heard it said of you that you can understand dreams and to interpret it. Joseph's expertise and understanding of dreams and interpretation was subjected to scrutiny. In the course of your duties, you may be called to question about your expertise, be ready to give everyone that asks you an answer satisfactorily.

A man that fears God does nothing hastily. So Joseph answered Pharaoh, saying it is not me, but God will give Pharaoh an answer of peace. He quickly brought to bear the Almighty God into the task ahead of him by acknowledging God as Omniscience and giver of wisdom and understanding.

"Trust in the Lord with all heart. And lean on your understanding. In all your ways acknowledged Him. And He shall direct your path." Prov. 3:5-6.

God opened Joseph's eyes of understanding and gave him divine wisdom and knowledge to provide a solution to the dreams. Pharaoh told Joseph all his dreams. Then Joseph replied to Pharaoh, saying his dreams were one and he revealed to Pharaoh what God was about to do. He then gave the interpretation of the dreams of how there will be seven years of abundance of food and another seven years of famine, he also provided a solution by advising Pharaoh to set discerning and wise men to gather food in the years of plenty against the impending seven years of great famine. The interpretation and solution pleased Pharaoh; said to his servants can we find, such as one as this man who is in the spirit of God? (Gen 41:38). Then Pharaoh said to Joseph, inasmuch as God has shown you all this, there is no one as discerning and wise as you. This was the time for Joseph to be decorated with medals.

Pharaoh declared, "You shall be over my house, and all my people shall be ruled according to your word, only in regard to the throne will I be greater than you." And Pharaoh said to Joseph see, "I have set you over all the land of Egypt." Then Pharaoh took his signet ring off his hand and put it on Joseph's hand and he clothed him in garments of fine lines and put a gold chain around his neck. Joseph's promotion and decoration with medals was signed and sealed. In addition to the promotion, he had Joseph to ride in the second chariot which he had, and they cried out before him and bowed on their knees! So he set him over all the land of Egypt. Pharaoh also said to Joseph, "I am Pharaoh and without your consent no man may lift his hand or foot in all the land of Egypt."

What an honor! Even Portiphat that sent him to prison, becomes a subject to him. Even his brothers that sold him into slavery eventually bowed to him. When God has penciled you for the honor, no one can disannul it, provided you did not wander away from His presence, but hold firmly to Him and follow after God. Though the journey might be rough and difficult, as long as you are determined to carry out your given assignment in the fear of the Lord and discharge your duties faithfully; the same God that took Joseph from prison to palace is still alive. He will teach you, instruct and guide you with His eyes as you walk through the pathway to honor until you are decorated with medals.

Japhthah is another man of honor, but he was a child of circumstance, coming out from such an unholy alliance. He grew up in the midst of his half-brothers, which later ganged-up against him, saying you have no part to inherit from our father's property. Claiming that he was a child of a harlot, eventually he was expelled from his father's house, thereby throwing him into the winds of life, for an offense he knew nothing about. When he fled from his brothers, he went to the land of 'Tob' (e.g. meaning good land) and worthless men gathered themselves together unto him raided from one place to another, training the street boys with the skill to prosecute war and his fame went abroad. Jephthah's only key into the word of God was in the book of Psalm.

"When my father and my mother forsake me, then the LORD will take care of me." Psalm 27:10.

In the process of time, the children of Ammon invaded Gilead confronting them to vacate the land now occupied by them, claiming that the land belonged to them, threatening the Israelite to either return the land in peace or face an impending war. When their ill-treatment was becoming unbearable for the Israelites, the elders of Gilead decided to seek help from Jephthah whom they have heard about his expertise in fighting a war. The issue confronting Gilead forced them to return to Jephthah. The stone which the builder rejected has become the 'head of the corner'.

They summoned up courage to meet with Jephthah requesting him to become their Commander to fight against the children of Ammon. Jephthah reminded the Elders of Gilead about their earlier treatment of him when they joined forces together to expel him from his father's house. "Why have you come to me now that you are in distress?" he queried? After much persuasion from the

Elders to forgive and forget the past and assist them to fight the children of Ammon Jephthah did not only agree, but he spelt out his own terms of reference which the Elders must agree to before joining them to fight the children of Ammon.

Thereby saying, if the Lord deliver the children of Ammon into his hand will the Elders of Gilead make him their head. The Elders made a vow that God bear them witness if they failed to do according to Jephthah's word. Jephthah then sent a message to the King of Ammon to refrain from his pursuit that the land which the people of Gilead are dwelling absolutely belongs to them.

After several attempts to make the King of Ammon see reason proved abortive, Jephthah then brought the Almighty God into the scene; thereby making a vow unto God that if He will deliver the people of Ammon into his hand, on his returning from the battlefield, he would sacrifice to God whatsoever comes out first from his house as a sign of gratitude to God. Because of the refusal of the King of Ammon to repent of his evil devices against the people of God (e.g. Israelite) the spirit of God descended upon Jephthah. He then draws the battle line with the children of Ammon. Because God was with him in the battle, he was victorious.

On his return from the battlefield with drumming and dancing with victorious song, approaching his house, his only daughter rushed out to welcome him with dancing. He remembered the vow he made unto God, his face became blooming, he toned his cloth and put ashes on his head, but his daughter encouraged him to keep his vow with the Lord. As a man of honor, he eventually kept his vow. At a later day, according to the request of her daughter, promise made, was a promise kept. As a man of integrity you must honor your word and promises always either to God or man.

He was appreciated by his people and decorated with medals. What an enduring honor indeed! An outcast became the head of a nation. No one else can do this except God Almighty. It was recorded in the Bible that Jephthah ruled over Israel for six years and died, and was given a state burial and finally buried in one of the great cities. This is a perfect example that true and enduring honor comes from God.

What about Jabez who was tagged with the name 'sorrow' from birth? The mother aggravated his predicament when she called his name Jabez. He grew up with this undesirable name, though he was more honorable than his brothers with a stigma. Jabez (e.g. Sorrow) He was seriously in need of change in his life, because no one wants to associate with sorrow. He called upon the name of God of Israel for an intervention, saying, "Oh, that you would bless me indeed and enlarge my territory, that your hands will be with me and deliver me from evil, that I may not cause pain to others." The mother said she gave him the name because I bore in pain and sorrow. What a mighty God we serve. He always uses the unwanted materials to confound the wise. So God granted him what he requested. Jabez simply anchored his faith upon the word in the psalmist.

"Call upon Me in the day of trouble; I will deliver you, and you shall glorify Me." Psalm 50:15.

Jabez wanted his situation to change for better. God actually enlarged his territory and he was more honorable than his brethren. Because he followed after God, he was eventually decorated with medals.

David, another man of honor in whom God testified that he is a man after His own heart, was a shepherd boy who was dutiful and faithful in his given assigned responsibility. At the time appointed he was being sought for right inside the wilderness to be honored.

Then the Lord called to Samuel, saying, "How long will you mourn for Saul, seeing I have rejected him from reigning over Israel? Fill your horn with oil now and go. I am sending you to house of Jesse the Bethlehemite, for I have provided myself a king among his sons." Samuel did according to the word of the Lord, he told Jesse to sanctify himself with his children and come with him to sacrifice.

So it was when they came that he looked at Eliab and said, "Surely the Lord's anointed is before him." But the Lord said to Samuel, "Don't look at his appearance or at his physical stature, because I have refused him. For the Lord does not see as men sees. For a man looks at the outward appearance, but the Lord looks at the hearts." Jesse called all his seven sons to pass before Samuel but no one was chosen. Then Samuel said to Jesse, "Are all the young men here?" Then said Jesse, "There remains yet the youngest and there he was keeping the sheep in the wilderness." Samuel asked Jesse to send and bring him for we will not sit down till he come here. So he sent and brought David to him, he was ruddy with bright eyes, and good-looking. The Lord said, "Arise, anoint him, for this is the one." Then Samuel took the horn of oil and anointed him in the midst of his brothers and the Spirit of the Lord came upon David from that day forward. Those that the Lord had assigned to help us to the place of honor would not rest until we are located and decorated with medals in Jesus Name amen.

So David was finally decorated with medals when he was anointed to rule over Israel. Then the tribes of Israel came to David at Hebron and spoke, saying indeed we are your bone and your flesh.

Also in the time past, when Saul was king over us, you were the one who led Israel out and brought them in and the Lord said to you, you shall shepherd my people Israel, and be a ruler over Israel. What an enduring honor indeed! It is not to be sought from men, because it is God who confers on people last and enduring honor. So in Hebron before the Lord, David was decorated as a king over Israel. He was thirty years old when he began to reign in Hebron. He reigned over Judah for seven years and six months and in Jerusalem, he reigned thirty-three years over all Israel and Judah. A great honor indeed!

These men of honor made it to God's own list of men of honor and at the time appointed they were decorated with medals along with other men of honor as recorded in the book of Hebrew: **"And what more shall I say? For time would fail me to tell of "Gideon and Barak and Samson and Jephthah, also David and Samuel and the prophets." Heb. 11:32.**

Friends, if you are a man of humble spirit, faithful and loyal, obedient, with the fear of God in your heart, living a righteous life, with the bowel of mercies, you are courageous having inborn desires to impact others and always time conscious. Assuredly you will be decorated with medals at the time appointed, if you stray not away from His presence.

If you strictly adhere to the principles enumerated in this book, He will lead you to a platform of desire where you shall be honored in Jesus Name.

Finally, my dear readers, God Almighty is the one who truly honors, not men, and He is the one to look up to for lasting and enduring honor. The pathway to that honor may seem to lead to nowhere and you MAY NOT KNOW WHAT GOD IS DOING, BUT GOD SURELY DOES KNOW WHAT HE IS DOING. Therefore, your constant obedience and faithfulness in all your undertaking will take you to your level of desire.

Please remember this always as your reference point: **"If you would earnestly seek God. And make your supplication to the Almighty, if you were pure and upright. Surely now He would awake for you. And prosper, your rightful dwelling place. Though your beginning was small, yet your later end would increase abundantly." Prov. 8:5-6.**

As you desire to be honored, hold firmly to the Almighty God. Surely you shall be decorated in Jesus Name.

"BE DECORATED WITH MEDALS"

Endeavour to practice the following words always.

1. "What your hand finds to do, do it with your might, for there is no work or device or knowledge or wisdom in the grave where you are going." Ecclesiastes 9:10&11.
2. "If the ax is dull, and one does not sharpen the edge. Then he must use strength. But wisdom brings success." Ecclesiastes 10:10.
3. In the morning sow your seed, and in the evening do not withhold your hand; for you do not know which will prosper; either this or that or whether both alike will be good." Ecclesiastes 11: 6.

Let's make this declaration:

1. I CONFESS to God that I am a sinner and believe that the Lord Jesus Christ died for my sins on the cross and was raised for my justification. I do now receive Him as my personal Lord and savior.

2. Stand fast therefore in the liberty by which Christ has made us free, and do not be entangled again with a "yoke of bondage". Galatians 5:1. You shall be decorated with medals. Shalom.

Emmanuel O. Afolabi

Tel: 0805-712-0673

0818-868-0576

Email: Emmanuelintererst05@yahoo.com,

Emmanuelafolabi2@gmail.com

Postal Address: P.O. Box 2048 Apapa, Lagos state, Nigeria.

ABOUT THE BOOK

On several occasions, I have been opportune to work closely with the author and have found out the he is a fine Christian, hardworking, a man of great honor and no wonder he is writing about the virtue of honor.

He is very articulate and very good when it comes to the work of God. Honor is not given, but it is acquired through hard work and humility. The writer of this book tries to admonish his readers to always seek the honor from God rather than man. This is the biblical standard and it's the one that a good Christian should seek after.

Honor from men does not always last and it is always bedeviled with strings. It is only God that gives the blessing without attaching strings to it. Men will always expect something in return for any good done.

The writer also tries to enumerate the ways to acquire godly honor and the possible pitfalls one should avoid in the quest for godly honor.

Honor is a virtue everybody should seek after because godly honor brings respect and makes way for anyone that rightly has it. I have no doubt that when you read through this book it will impart your life positively and makes you a man of honor indeed.

"I therefore recommend to you this book, The Pathway to Honor, as a book you must read." ~ Pastor Percy O. Adekanle, Resident Pastor of Foursquare Gospel Church in Nigeria; Jakande Zonal Headquarters Church

AUTHOR BIOGRAPHY

Emmanuel O. Afolabi has held several positions in many branches of the Foursquare Gospel Church in Nigeria since his salvation over three decades ago. He has worked in the Christian Education Department where he was once the Discipleship Superintendent, Assistant General Sunday School Superintendent, for many years amongst others. At present, he is the General Sunday school Superintendent and Church Secretary of Foursquare Gospel Church, Ishoru Estate, Bucknor, Ejigbo, Lagos State. He was formerly the Purchasing Manager/Clearing Officer of Fare-east Merchandise Company, Ltd. and Panalpina World Transport (Nig.) Ltd. He is married and blessed with children to the glory of God.

www.ingramcontent.com/pod-product-compliance
Lightning Source LLC
Chambersburg PA
CBHW052120070526
44584CB00017B/2568